GO PROGRAM

I0012744

FOR WEB DEVELOPERS

OLIVER LUCAS JR

TABLE OF CONTENTS

Chapter 1

Chapter 2

Chapter 3

Chapter 4

Chapter 5

Chapter 6

Chapter 7

Chapter 8

Chapter 9

Chapter 10

Preface

Welcome to **"Go Programming for Web Developers"**! This book is your comprehensive guide to building modern, efficient, and scalable web applications using the Go programming language. Whether you're a seasoned web developer exploring Go for the first time or a newcomer eager to dive into the world of web development, this book will equip you with the knowledge and skills you need to succeed.

Go, often referred to as Golang, has emerged as a powerful language for web development due to its unique blend of speed, simplicity, and concurrency. Its clear syntax, robust standard library, and built-in support for concurrency make it an ideal choice for creating high-performance web applications.

This book takes a practical, hands-on approach to learning Go for web development. We'll start with the fundamentals of the language and gradually progress to more advanced topics, covering everything from handling HTTP requests and working with databases to building RESTful APIs and securing your applications. Throughout the book, you'll find numerous examples, code snippets, and mini-projects to reinforce your learning and help you build real-world web applications.

Here's what you'll learn:

Fundamentals of Go: Master the essential syntax, data structures, and control flow of the Go language.

Web Development with Go: Learn how to handle HTTP requests, serve static files, and build dynamic web pages using templates.

Databases and Go: Connect to SQL databases, perform CRUD operations, and explore Object-Relational Mapping (ORM) with GORM.

RESTful APIs: Design and build RESTful APIs, handle JSON data, and implement authentication and authorization.

Go Web Frameworks: Explore popular Go web frameworks like Gin, Echo, and Fiber, and learn how to leverage their features to build efficient web applications.

Testing and Debugging: Write unit tests for your Go web code and master debugging techniques to identify and resolve issues effectively.

Deployment and Scaling: Deploy your Go web applications to servers, including cloud platforms and Docker containers, and learn how to scale your applications for high traffic and performance.

Who is this book for?

This book is for anyone who wants to learn how to build web applications with Go, including:

Web developers with experience in other languages (e.g., Python, JavaScript, Ruby) who want to explore Go.

Backend developers who want to expand their skillset and learn a new language for building web applications.

Students and beginners who are passionate about web development and want to start with a powerful and efficient language.

How to use this book:

This book is designed to be read sequentially, as each chapter builds upon the concepts introduced in the previous ones. However, you can also use it as a reference guide, jumping to specific sections as needed. The code examples in the book are available online, allowing you to experiment and modify them to further your learning.

We encourage you to actively engage with the material, write code, and build your own projects as you progress through the book. The best way to learn Go for web development is by doing!

We hope this book empowers you to create amazing web applications with Go. Let's get started!

Chapter 1

Welcome to the Go Web

1.1 Why Go for Web Development? (Speed, Concurrency, Simplicity)

Go has rapidly become a popular choice for web development, and this section should highlight the key reasons why it's so well-suited for this purpose. Here's a breakdown of those reasons:

Speed:

Go is a compiled language, meaning the code is translated directly into machine code before execution. This results in significantly faster performance compared to interpreted languages like Python or Ruby, where code is interpreted at runtime.

Go's efficient garbage collection and memory management further contribute to its speed, minimizing pauses and maximizing resource utilization.

This speed translates to faster response times for web applications, which is crucial for a good user experience and SEO.

Concurrency:

Go has built-in concurrency features through goroutines and channels. Goroutines are lightweight, independently executing functions that allow a program to handle multiple tasks concurrently. Channels provide a safe and efficient way for goroutines to communicate and synchronize.

This makes Go ideal for building web applications that need to handle many concurrent requests, such as high-traffic websites, real-time applications, and APIs.

Go's concurrency model is easier to use and understand compared to traditional threading models, reducing the complexity of concurrent programming.

Simplicity:

Go has a clean and concise syntax, making it easy to learn and read. This reduces development time and makes it easier to maintain and debug code.

Go's standard library is comprehensive and well-documented, providing ready-to-use packages for common web development tasks like handling HTTP requests, working with databases, and encoding/decoding JSON.

Go's focus on simplicity leads to more robust and reliable web applications with fewer errors and vulnerabilities.

In this section, it would be helpful to include:

Benchmarks: Show some performance comparisons between Go and other languages in web server scenarios.

Examples: Provide simple code examples that demonstrate Go's concurrency in action, like handling multiple requests simultaneously.

Case Studies: Mention companies or projects that use Go for their web applications (e.g., Google, Dropbox, Docker) and highlight the benefits they've experienced.

By effectively conveying these advantages, you'll convince your readers that Go is a powerful and efficient language for web development.

1.2   Setting Up Your Go Environment (Installation, Tools, First Program)

1. Installation:

Download: Direct readers to the official Go website (golang.org) to download the appropriate installer for their operating system (Windows, macOS, Linux).

Installation process: Provide clear instructions for each OS, including screenshots or screencasts if possible.

For Windows and macOS, this typically involves running the installer and following the prompts.

For Linux, readers might need to extract a tarball and set up environment variables.

Verification: Show readers how to verify the installation by opening a terminal or command prompt and running the command `go version`. This should display the installed Go version.

2. Tools:

Text Editor/IDE: Recommend a suitable code editor or IDE for Go development. Popular choices include:

VS Code: A free, lightweight editor with excellent Go support through the official Go extension.

GoLand: A full-featured IDE from JetBrains specifically designed for Go development.

Sublime Text: A versatile text editor with good Go support through plugins.

The `go` **command:** Introduce the essential `go` commands for building, running, and managing Go projects:

`go run`: Run a Go program.

`go build`: Compile a Go program into an executable.

`go get`: Download and install Go packages.

`go test`: Run tests for a Go package.

Debugging tools: Briefly mention debugging tools like Delve, which can be used to step through code, inspect variables, and find errors.

3. First Program:

"Hello, world!": Guide readers through writing a simple "Hello, world!" program in Go. This introduces the basic structure of a Go program:

Go

```go
package main

import "fmt"

func main() {
    fmt.Println("Hello, world!")
}
```

Explanation: Explain each line of code:

`package main`: Indicates that this is the main program file.

`import "fmt"`: Imports the `fmt` package for printing output.

`func main()`: The main function where the program execution begins.

`fmt.Println("Hello, world!")`: Prints the "Hello, world!" message to the console.

Running the program: Show readers how to save the code as a `.go` file (e.g., `hello.go`) and run it using `go run hello.go`.

Important Considerations:

Environment variables: Clearly explain the purpose of environment variables like `GOROOT` (Go installation directory) and `GOPATH` (workspace directory). Provide step-by-step instructions on how to set them correctly for each operating system.

Troubleshooting: Include common installation issues and their solutions.

Go Modules: Introduce Go modules as the modern way to manage dependencies in Go projects.

1.3 Essential Go Syntax for Web Developers (Variables, Functions, Control Flow)

This section provides a foundational understanding of Go syntax, focusing on the elements most relevant to web development.

1. Variables:

Declaration: Go uses the `var` keyword to declare variables. You specify the variable name and its data type (e.g., `var age int`, `var name string`).

Type inference: Go can often infer the data type of a variable based on the value assigned to it. This allows for shorter declarations using `:=` (e.g., `age := 25`, `name := "Alice"`).

Common data types: Introduce the data types commonly used in web development:

`int`: For storing integers (e.g., user IDs, product quantities).

`string`: For storing text (e.g., names, emails, URLs).

`bool`: For storing boolean values (true/false) (e.g., user login status, feature flags).

`float64`: For storing floating-point numbers (e.g., prices, ratings).

2. Functions:

Definition: Functions are declared using the `func` keyword, followed by the function name, parameters, and return type (e.g., `func add(x int, y int) int`).

Parameters: Functions can accept parameters as input, allowing you to pass data into them.

Return values: Functions can return values, allowing you to get data back from them.

Built-in functions: Go provides many useful built-in functions, such as:

`len()`: Returns the length of a string or array.

`print()`: Prints output to the console.

`strconv.Atoi()`: Converts a string to an integer.

3. Control Flow:

Conditional statements (`if`, `else if`, `else`): Allow you to execute different blocks of code based on conditions (e.g., `if age >= 18 { // allow access } else { // deny access }`).

Loops (`for`): Allow you to repeat a block of code multiple times (e.g., `for i := 0; i < 10; i++ { // do something }`).

Switch statements: Provide an efficient way to handle multiple conditions (e.g., `switch day { case "Monday": // ...` `case "Tuesday": // ... }`).

Important Considerations:

Code style: Introduce Go's coding conventions, such as using camelCase for variable names and adding comments to explain your code.

Error handling: Briefly touch on error handling using `if err != nil` checks.

Best practices: Emphasize the importance of writing clean, readable, and maintainable code.

Chapter 2

Building Blocks: Handling HTTP Requests

2.1 Understanding HTTP and the Request/Response Cycle

This section dives into the core of how web communication works, introducing the Hypertext Transfer Protocol (HTTP) and its request/response cycle.

1. What is HTTP?

Definition: HTTP is the foundation of data exchange on the World Wide Web. It's a protocol that defines how clients (like web browsers) request resources from servers (where websites are hosted).

Client-Server Model: Explain the client-server architecture, where clients initiate requests and servers respond with the requested resources or information.

Statelessness: HTTP is a stateless protocol, meaning each request is treated independently. The server doesn't retain any memory of previous requests from the same client.

2. The Request/Response Cycle:

Request:

A client sends an HTTP request to a server, specifying the desired action (e.g., retrieve a web page, submit data).

The request includes:

Method: Indicates the action to be performed (e.g., `GET`, `POST`, `PUT`, `DELETE`).

URL: Specifies the address of the resource.

Headers: Contains metadata about the request (e.g., browser type, accepted languages).

Body: Optional data sent with the request (e.g., form data).

Response:

The server processes the request and sends back an HTTP response.

The response includes:

Status Code: Indicates the outcome of the request (e.g., `200 OK`, `404 Not Found`).

Headers: Contains metadata about the response (e.g., content type, server information).

Body: The actual content being sent back (e.g., HTML, JSON, image data).

3. HTTP Methods:

GET: Retrieves data from the server.

POST: Submits data to be processed by the server (e.g., form submissions).

PUT: Updates an existing resource on the server.

DELETE: Deletes a resource on the server.

4. HTTP Status Codes:

1xx: Informational (e.g., `100 Continue`).

2xx: Success (e.g., `200 OK`, `201 Created`).

3xx: Redirection (e.g., `301 Moved Permanently`, `302 Found`).

4xx: Client Error (e.g., `400 Bad Request`, `404 Not Found`).

5xx: Server Error (e.g., `500 Internal Server Error`, `503 Service Unavailable`).

Visual Aids:

Include diagrams or flowcharts to illustrate the client-server interaction and the steps in the request/response cycle.

Show examples of HTTP requests and responses using tools like `curl` or by inspecting network requests in a web browser's developer tools.

2.2 Serving Static Files and Building a Simple Web Server

This section provides a practical introduction to serving static files, a fundamental aspect of web development.

1. What are Static Files?

Definition: Static files are the unchanging components of a website, such as:

HTML files: Provide the structure and content of web pages.

CSS files: Define the styling and visual presentation.

JavaScript files: Add interactivity and dynamic behavior.

Images: Visual elements like photos, illustrations, and icons.

Importance: Static files are essential for any website, forming the foundation of its appearance and user interface.

2. Serving Static Files with `http.FileServer`:

`http.FileServer`: Go's `net/http` package provides a convenient way to serve static files from a directory using the `http.FileServer` function.

`http.Dir`: `http.Dir` is used to convert a string representing a directory path into an `http.FileSystem` value, which `http.FileServer` can then use to serve files.

Example:

Go

```
import (
    "net/http"
)

func main() {
    fs := http.FileServer(http.Dir("static")) //
Serve files from the "static" directory
                        http.Handle("/static/",
http.StripPrefix("/static/",   fs))   //  Map   the
"/static/" URL path to the file server
    http.ListenAndServe(":8080", nil)
}
```

3. Building a Simple Web Server:

Project Structure: Guide readers through creating a basic project structure:

Create a project directory (e.g., `my-web-server`).

Create a `static` directory inside the project directory to store static files (HTML, CSS, images).

Create a `main.go` file in the project directory to write the Go code.

HTML File: Create a simple `index.html` file in the `static` directory with basic HTML content.

Go Code: Write the Go code to serve the `index.html` file from the `static` directory using `http.FileServer`.

4. Key Considerations:

File Paths: Explain the importance of using relative file paths to ensure the server can locate the files correctly.

Error Handling: Show how to handle potential errors when opening files or directories.

Security: Emphasize the need to avoid serving sensitive files or directories.

Example Project Structure:

```
my-web-server/
├── static/
│      └── index.html
└── main.go
```

By the end of this section, readers should be able to build a simple web server that serves static files, laying the foundation for more complex web applications.

Chapter 3

Dynamic Content with Templates

3.1 Introduction to HTML Templating in Go

This section introduces the concept of HTML templating and its importance in Go web development.

1. Why Templates?

Separation of Concerns: Templates help separate the presentation layer (HTML) from the application logic (Go code). This makes your code cleaner, easier to maintain, and more readable.

Reusability: Templates allow you to define reusable components and layouts, reducing code duplication and ensuring consistency across your web application.

Dynamic Content: Templates enable you to generate dynamic HTML pages by combining static content with data from your Go code. This allows you to personalize content, display data from databases, and create interactive features.

2. Go's `html/template` Package:

Built-in Solution: Go provides a powerful and secure templating engine through the `html/template` package in its standard library.

Key Features:

Data Evaluation: Access and display data passed from your Go code within the HTML.

Control Structures: Use conditional statements (`if`, `else`) and loops (`range`) to create dynamic content.

Functions: Call built-in and custom functions to format and process data within the template.

Security: Automatic escaping of data to prevent cross-site scripting (XSS) vulnerabilities.

3. Basic Template Syntax:

`{{ }}`: Delimiters used to embed Go code or data within the HTML template.

`.`: Represents the current data context within the template.

Example: `<h1>Welcome, {{ .Name }}!</h1>` - This would display a heading with the user's name, assuming the data passed to the template has a `Name` field.

4. Creating and Parsing Templates:

`template.New()`: Creates a new template object.

`template.ParseFiles()`: Parses one or more template files (typically with a `.gohtml` extension) and adds them to the template object.

`template.Execute()`: Executes the template, combining it with the provided data and writing the output to a writer (e.g., an `http.ResponseWriter`).

Example:

Go

```
import (

    "html/template"

    "net/http"
```

```go
)

func      handler(w       http.ResponseWriter,      r
*http.Request) {

                                      tmpl            :=
template.Must(template.ParseFiles("templates/inde
x.gohtml"))

    data := struct{ Name string }{Name: "Alice"}

    tmpl.Execute(w, data)

}
```

This code snippet demonstrates how to parse a template file (`templates/index.gohtml`) and execute it with a simple data structure to generate dynamic HTML.

3.2   Working   with   Go's `html/template` Package

This section explores the features and capabilities of Go's `html/template` package in more detail, showing readers how to create dynamic and engaging web pages.

1. Template Actions:

Data Evaluation: Access and display data from your Go code within the template using the . (dot) notation. For example, `{{ .Name }}` would output the value of the `Name` field from the data passed to the template.

Conditional Logic: Use `{{ if }}`, `{{ else if }}`, and `{{ else }}` actions to conditionally render parts of the template based on data or conditions.

Loops: Iterate over arrays, slices, and maps using the `{{ range }}` action. This allows you to dynamically generate lists, tables, or other repetitive elements.

Functions: Call built-in template functions (e.g., `len`, `index`, `printf`) or define your own custom functions in Go to perform operations on data within the template.

Pipelines: Chain multiple actions together using the `|` (pipe) operator. This allows you to modify data before outputting it, such as formatting a date or truncating a string.

2. Template Functions:

Custom Functions: Define functions in your Go code and make them available to your templates using `template.Funcs()`. These functions can take arguments and return values, allowing you to perform complex logic within the template.

Example:

Go

```go
func formatDate(t time.Time) string {

    return t.Format("January 2, 2006")

}



func main() {
```

```
                                    tmpl         :=
template.Must(template.New("index").Funcs(templat
e.FuncMap{

        "formatDate": formatDate,

    }).ParseFiles("templates/index.gohtml"))

    // ...

}
```

3. Template Inheritance and Inclusion:

Inheritance: Create base templates with common layouts and elements (e.g., header, footer) and then define child templates that inherit from the base template and override specific sections.

Inclusion: Include smaller templates within larger ones using the `{{ template "templateName" }}` action. This promotes modularity and reusability.

4. Handling User Input and Security:

Automatic Escaping: `html/template` automatically escapes data to prevent cross-site scripting (XSS) attacks. This ensures that user-generated content is displayed safely in the HTML.

Contextual Escaping: Use the `html` and `js` template actions to explicitly control escaping in specific contexts (e.g., when including user-generated content within HTML attributes or JavaScript code).

Example (Inheritance):

base.gohtml:

HTML

```
<!DOCTYPE html>

<html>

<head>

    <title>{{ .Title }}</title>

</head>

<body>

    {{ block "content" . }} {{ end }}

</body>

</html>
```

index.gohtml:

HTML

```
{{ define "content" }}

    <h1>Welcome to my website!</h1>

{{ end }}
```

This demonstrates how to define a base template with a `content` block and a child template that defines the content within that block.

3.3 Data Structures and Template Functions

This section focuses on how data interacts with Go templates, enabling you to create dynamic web pages that display information from your Go code.

1. Passing Data to Templates:

Structs: Go's structs are a powerful way to organize data. You can define structs to represent the information you want to display in your templates (e.g., a `User` struct with fields like `Name`, `Email`, and `Age`).

`template.Execute()`: When executing a template with `template.Execute()`, you pass an instance of your data structure as the second argument. This makes the data accessible within the template.

2. Accessing Data in Templates:

Dot Notation: Inside the template, you can access the fields of your data structure using the `.` (dot) operator. For example, `{{ .Name }}` would access the `Name` field of the data passed to the template.

Nested Fields: You can access nested fields using chained dot notation. For example, if your data structure has a field `User` which itself has a field `Name`, you can access it with `{{ .User.Name }}`.

3. Template Functions for Data Manipulation:

`template.Funcs()`: You can define custom functions in your Go code and make them available to your templates using `template.Funcs()`. These functions can be used to format data, perform calculations, or make decisions within the template.

Example:

Go

```go
func formatDate(t time.Time) string {

    return t.Format("January 2, 2006")

}



func main() {

    // ...

    tmpl := template.Must(template.New("index").Funcs(template.FuncMap{

        "formatDate": formatDate,

    }).ParseFiles("templates/index.gohtml"))

    // ...

}
```

In your template, you could then use `{{ formatDate .Date }}` to format a date field.

4. Working with Different Data Structures:

Arrays and Slices: You can iterate over arrays and slices using the `{{ range }}` action. This allows you to dynamically generate lists or tables of data.

Maps: You can access values in maps by key using `{{ .MapName.KeyName }}`.

5. Conditional Logic with Data:

`if`, `else if`, `else`: You can use conditional actions in your templates to display content based on data values. For example, you could show a welcome message only if the user is logged in.

Example (Data Structure and Template):

Go Code:

```go
Go
type Product struct {

    Name   string

    Price  float64

}



func       handler(w       http.ResponseWriter,       r
*http.Request) {

    // ...

    products := []Product{

        {Name: "Shirt", Price: 25.99},
```

```
        {Name: "Shoes", Price: 79.99},

    }

    tmpl.Execute(w, products)

}
```

Template (index.gohtml):

HTML

```html
<h1>Products</h1>

<ul>

    {{ range . }}

        <li>{{ .Name }} - ${{ .Price }}</li>

    {{ end }}

</ul>
```

This example demonstrates how to pass a slice of `Product` structs to a template and iterate over it to display a list of products.

Chapter 4

Working with Forms and User Input

4.1 Handling HTML Forms in Go

This section explores how to process user input from HTML forms in your Go web applications, allowing you to create interactive web pages.

1. HTML Forms Basics:

Purpose: HTML forms provide a way for users to input data that can be sent to your web server. This data can be used for various purposes, such as user login, contact forms, searches, and more.

Form Elements: Common form elements include:

`<form>`: The container for all form elements.

`<input>`: Used for various input types like text, password, email, submit buttons, etc.

`<textarea>`: For multi-line text input.

`<select>`: Creates dropdown lists.

`<button>`: Clickable buttons for submitting the form or performing other actions.

Attributes: Important form attributes include:

`action`: Specifies the URL where the form data will be sent.

`method`: Specifies the HTTP method to use for submitting the form (usually `GET` or `POST`).

2. Receiving Form Data in Go:

`net/http` **Package:** The `net/http` package provides tools for accessing form data sent to your Go web server.

`Request` **Object:** The `http.Request` object, passed to your handler functions, contains information about the incoming request, including form data.

Accessing Form Values:

`r.FormValue("fieldName")`: Retrieves the value of a specific form field with the given name.

`r.Form`: A map that holds all form data. You might need to call `r.ParseForm()` to parse the request body and populate this map.

3. Handling Different Form Elements:

Text Inputs and Textareas: Values can be retrieved directly using `r.FormValue()`.

Checkboxes: Check if a checkbox is selected by checking if `r.FormValue("checkboxName")` is not empty.

Radio Buttons: Retrieve the value of the selected radio button in a group.

Select Dropdowns: Get the value of the selected option.

4. Form Submission and Redirection:

Handling Submissions: In your Go handler function, process the received form data (e.g., validate it, store it in a database, send an email).

Redirection: After processing the form data, you can redirect the user to a different page using `http.Redirect()`. This is often used to display a "thank you" message or to redirect to a different part of the application.

Example:

Go

```go
func contactHandler(w http.ResponseWriter, r *http.Request) {

    if r.Method == http.MethodPost {

        r.ParseForm()

        name := r.FormValue("name")

        email := r.FormValue("email")

        message := r.FormValue("message")

        // ... process the form data (e.g., send an email) ...

        http.Redirect(w, r, "/thank-you", http.StatusSeeOther)

    } else {

        // ... display the contact form ...

    }

}
```

This example shows a handler function that processes a contact form submission, retrieves the form data, and redirects the user to a "thank you" page.

4.2 Processing Form Data and Validation

This section delves into the crucial steps after receiving form data: processing it and ensuring its validity before using it in your web application.

1. Data Processing:

Retrieval: Once you've received form data (as explained in the previous section), you need to extract the values from the `http.Request` object using `r.FormValue("fieldName")`.

Conversion: Often, form data is received as strings. You might need to convert it to other data types (e.g., integers, floats, booleans) depending on how you intend to use it.

Storage: Process the data according to your application's logic. This might involve:

Storing it in a database.

Sending an email.

Performing calculations.

Generating dynamic content.

2. Data Validation:

Importance: Validation ensures that the data received from the user is in the correct format, within acceptable ranges, and meets any other requirements of your application. This prevents errors, improves data quality, and enhances security.

Validation Techniques:

Required Fields: Check if mandatory fields have been filled in.

Data Types: Ensure that data is of the correct type (e.g., an email address field should contain a valid email format).

Length: Check if the data meets length requirements (e.g., a password should be at least 8 characters long).

Range: Validate that numerical data falls within acceptable ranges (e.g., age should be a positive number).

Patterns: Use regular expressions to validate data against specific patterns (e.g., phone numbers, zip codes).

Error Handling: If validation fails, provide informative error messages to the user, guiding them to correct the input.

3. Go Libraries for Validation:

Validator.v9: This popular library provides a wide range of validation functions and allows you to define custom validation rules.

Example:

Go

```go
import (

    "github.com/go-playground/validator/v10"

)



type User struct {

    Name   string `validate:"required"`

    Email string `validate:"required,email"`

    Age    int    `validate:"gte=18"`

}
```

```go
func main() {

    validate := validator.New()

    user := User{Name: "Alice", Email:
"alice@example.com", Age: 25}

    err := validate.Struct(user)

    if err != nil {

        // Handle validation errors

    }

}
```

4. Best Practices:

Validate on Both Client and Server: Perform validation on the client-side (using JavaScript) for a better user experience and on the server-side (using Go) for security and data integrity.

Clear Error Messages: Provide specific and user-friendly error messages to guide the user in correcting their input.

Security: Be mindful of security vulnerabilities like cross-site scripting (XSS) when processing user input. Sanitize data to prevent malicious code injection.

4.3 Preventing Cross-Site Scripting (XSS)

1. What is Cross-Site Scripting (XSS)?

Definition: XSS is a security vulnerability that allows attackers to inject malicious scripts into web pages viewed by other users.

How it Works: Attackers exploit vulnerabilities in web applications to inject malicious code, typically JavaScript, into the website's output. When other users visit the affected page, their browsers execute the malicious script, which can:

Steal user cookies and session data.

Redirect users to phishing websites.

Modify the content of the website.

Access sensitive information.

Example: Imagine a website with a comment section. An attacker could submit a comment containing malicious JavaScript code. If the website doesn't properly sanitize the input, the code will be displayed on the page, and anyone who views the comment will have the script executed in their browser.

2. Preventing XSS in Go:

Output Encoding: The most effective way to prevent XSS is to encode user-generated content before displaying it on the web page. This converts special characters (like <, >, ") into their HTML entity equivalents (like `&lt;`, `&gt;`, `&quot;`), preventing them from being interpreted as code.

`html/template` **Package:** Go's `html/template` package provides automatic output encoding by default. This means that data passed to templates is automatically escaped, significantly reducing the risk of XSS.

Contextual Escaping: In situations where you need to include user-generated content in specific contexts (e.g., within HTML attributes or JavaScript code), use the `html/template` package's contextual escaping functions:

`{{ .Content | html }}`: Escapes content for use within HTML.

`{{ .Content | js }}`: Escapes content for use within JavaScript.

3. Best Practices:

Validate and Sanitize All Input: Always validate and sanitize any data received from users, even if you're using `html/template`. This adds an extra layer of security.

Use a Web Application Firewall (WAF): A WAF can help detect and block XSS attacks.

Stay Updated: Keep your Go version and any third-party libraries you use up-to-date to patch known vulnerabilities.

Security Headers: Use appropriate security headers like `Content-Security-Policy` to further mitigate XSS risks.

4. Example:

Go

```go
func commentHandler(w http.ResponseWriter, r *http.Request) {

    // ... get comment from user ...

    tmpl := template.Must(template.ParseFiles("templates/comments.gohtml"))

    data := struct{ Comment string }{Comment: comment}

    tmpl.Execute(w, data)
```

```
}
```

In the `comments.gohtml` template:

HTML

```
<p>{{ .Comment }}</p>
```

The `html/template` package will automatically escape any potentially harmful characters in the `Comment` before displaying it, preventing XSS.

Chapter 5

Databases and Go

5.1 Connecting to SQL Databases (PostgreSQL, MySQL)

This section provides a practical guide to connecting your Go web applications to popular SQL databases like PostgreSQL and MySQL.

1. Database Drivers:

`database/sql` **Package:** Go's standard library includes the `database/sql` package, which provides a generic interface for interacting with SQL databases.

Database-Specific Drivers: To connect to a specific database like PostgreSQL or MySQL, you need a database-specific driver that implements the `database/sql` interface. Popular drivers include:

PostgreSQL: `github.com/lib/pq`

MySQL: `github.com/go-sql-driver/mysql`

Installation: Show readers how to install these drivers using `go get`:

Bash

```
go get github.com/lib/pq

go get github.com/go-sql-driver/mysql
```

2. Connection Strings:

Format: A connection string provides the necessary information to connect to the database, including the database type, host, port, username, password, and database name.

Examples:

PostgreSQL:

```
postgres://username:password@host:port/database_n
ame?sslmode=disable
```

MySQL:

```
username:password@tcp(host:port)/database_name
```

Security: Emphasize the importance of storing database credentials securely, such as using environment variables or configuration files.

3. Connecting to the Database:

`sql.Open()`: Use the `sql.Open()` function to establish a connection to the database. This function takes the driver name and the connection string as arguments.

`db.Ping()`: Use `db.Ping()` to test the database connection.

Error Handling: Always handle potential errors that might occur during the connection process.

Example (PostgreSQL):

```go
Go

import (

    "database/sql"
```

```go
        _ "github.com/lib/pq" // Import the
PostgreSQL driver

)


func main() {

                            connStr      :=
"postgres://username:password@localhost:5432/myda
tabase?sslmode=disable"

    db, err := sql.Open("postgres", connStr)

    if err != nil {

        panic(err)

    }

    defer db.Close()


    err = db.Ping()

    if err != nil {

        panic(err)

    }

    // ... database connection successful ...

}
```

4. Connection Pooling:

Concept: Explain the benefits of connection pooling, which reuses existing database connections to improve performance and reduce overhead.

Go's `database/sql`: Go's `database/sql` package handles connection pooling automatically.

5. Best Practices:

Close Connections: Always close database connections when you're finished with them using `db.Close()`.

Prepared Statements: Use prepared statements to prevent SQL injection vulnerabilities.

Transactions: Use transactions to ensure data consistency when performing multiple database operations.

5.2 Using Go's `database/sql` Package

This section dives deeper into Go's `database/sql` package, exploring how to interact with SQL databases effectively.

1. Executing SQL Queries:

`db.Query()`: Use `db.Query()` to execute `SELECT` queries that return rows of data. This function returns a `*sql.Rows` object, which you can iterate over to retrieve the results.

`db.QueryRow()`: Use `db.QueryRow()` for queries that are expected to return a single row.

`db.Exec()`: Use `db.Exec()` to execute `INSERT`, `UPDATE`, and `DELETE` queries that don't return rows. This function returns a `sql.Result` object, which can be used to get information about the affected rows.

Example (Query):

Go

```go
rows, err := db.Query("SELECT id, name, email FROM users")

if err != nil {

    panic(err)

}

defer rows.Close()


for rows.Next() {

    var id int

    var name, email string

    err = rows.Scan(&id, &name, &email)

    if err != nil {

        panic(err)

    }

    fmt.Println(id, name, email)

}
```

2. Prepared Statements:

Concept: Prepared statements are pre-compiled SQL queries that can be executed multiple times with different parameters. They improve performance and prevent SQL injection vulnerabilities.

`db.Prepare()`: Use `db.Prepare()` to create a prepared statement.

`stmt.Exec()` / `stmt.Query()`: Use the `Exec()` or `Query()` methods of the prepared statement to execute it with the provided parameters.

Example:

Go

```go
stmt, err := db.Prepare("INSERT INTO users(name, email) VALUES($1, $2)")

if err != nil {

    panic(err)

}

defer stmt.Close()


_, err = stmt.Exec("Alice", "alice@example.com")

if err != nil {

    panic(err)

}
```

3. Transactions:

Concept: Transactions group multiple database operations into a single unit of work, ensuring that either all operations succeed or none do. This is crucial for maintaining data consistency.

`db.Begin()`: Start a transaction using `db.Begin()`.

`tx.Exec()` **/** `tx.Query()`: Execute queries within the transaction using the transaction object (`tx`).

`tx.Commit()` **/** `tx.Rollback()`: Commit the transaction using `tx.Commit()` if all operations are successful, or rollback the transaction using `tx.Rollback()` if an error occurs.

Example:

Go

```go
tx, err := db.Begin()

if err != nil {

    panic(err)

}



_, err = tx.Exec("INSERT INTO users(name, email) VALUES($1, $2)", "Bob", "bob@example.com")

if err != nil {

    tx.Rollback()

    panic(err)

}
```

```
_, err = tx.Exec("UPDATE products SET quantity =
quantity - 1 WHERE id = $1", 123)

if err != nil {

    tx.Rollback()

    panic(err)

}


err = tx.Commit()

if err != nil {

    panic(err)

}
```

4. Error Handling:

`sql.ErrNoRows`: Handle the specific case where a query doesn't return any rows using `sql.ErrNoRows`.

Other Errors: Handle other potential errors, such as connection errors or query errors, gracefully.

5. Best Practices:

Use Named Parameters: Use named parameters in prepared statements for better readability and maintainability.

Context with Timeouts: Use context with timeouts to prevent long-running queries from blocking your application.

5.3 Object-Relational Mapping (ORM) with GORM

This section introduces Object-Relational Mapping (ORM) and how it simplifies database interactions in Go web applications using the popular GORM library.

1. What is ORM?

Concept: ORM is a technique that allows you to interact with your database using objects and methods instead of writing raw SQL queries. It bridges the gap between your object-oriented Go code and the relational database.

Benefits:

Increased Productivity: Write less code and focus on your application logic.

Improved Maintainability: Cleaner and more organized code.

Enhanced Security: ORMs often provide protection against SQL injection vulnerabilities.

Database Independence: Switch between different database systems more easily.

2. GORM - The Go ORM Library:

Introduction: GORM is a popular and feature-rich ORM library for Go. It provides a developer-friendly way to interact with various SQL databases (PostgreSQL, MySQL, SQLite, etc.).

Installation:

Bash

```
go get gorm.io/gorm
```

```
go get gorm.io/driver/postgres // Or your
preferred database driver
```

3. Defining Models:

Structs as Models: In GORM, you define your database tables as Go structs. Each field in the struct corresponds to a column in the table.

GORM Tags: Use GORM tags to specify constraints, data types, and other properties of the database columns.

Example:

Go

```
type User struct {

        gorm.Model // Includes ID, CreatedAt,
UpdatedAt, DeletedAt

    Name   string `gorm:"size:255"`

    Email string `gorm:"uniqueIndex;size:255"`

}
```

4. Basic Operations with GORM:

Creating a Record: `db.Create(&user)`

Retrieving Records: `db.First(&user, 1)` (finds user with ID 1)

Updating Records: `db.Model(&user).Update("Name", "John Doe")`

Deleting Records: `db.Delete(&user)`

Where Clauses: `db.Where("name = ?", "Alice").Find(&users)`

5. Relationships:

Defining Relationships: GORM supports various relationships between models (one-to-one, one-to-many, many-to-many).

Example (One-to-Many):

```Go
type User struct {

    // ...

    Posts []Post

}


type Post struct {

    gorm.Model

    UserID uint

    Title    string
```

```
Content string

}
```

6. Advanced Features:

Callbacks: Execute code before or after create, update, delete operations.

Hooks: Fine-grained control over database operations.

Preloading: Eagerly load related data to improve performance.

Transactions: Ensure data consistency for multiple operations.

7. Best Practices:

Database Migrations: Use GORM's migration features to manage database schema changes.

Indexes: Create indexes on frequently queried columns to improve performance.

Error Handling: Handle potential GORM errors gracefully.

By introducing GORM and its features, your readers will be able to leverage the power of ORM to simplify database interactions and build more efficient and maintainable Go web applications.

Chapter 6

Building RESTful APIs

6.1 Understanding RESTful API Design Principles

1. What is REST?

Architectural Style: REST is not a strict standard but rather a set of architectural principles for designing networked applications.

Focus on Resources: RESTful APIs revolve around resources, which are any entities that can be identified and accessed (e.g., users, products, articles).

Uniform Interface: RESTful APIs use standard HTTP methods (`GET`, `POST`, `PUT`, `DELETE`) to interact with resources.

2. Key Principles of REST:

Client-Server: Separation of concerns between the client (consumer of the API) and the server (provider of the API).

Statelessness: Each request from the client must contain all the information necessary for the server to understand and process it. The server does not store any client context between requests.

Cacheability: Responses from the server should explicitly state whether they can be cached or not, allowing clients to reuse responses and improve performance.

Uniform Interface: This is a fundamental principle of REST, emphasizing a consistent way to interact with resources through:

Identification of resources: Resources are identified by URIs (Uniform Resource Identifiers).

Manipulation of resources through representations: Clients interact with representations of resources (e.g., JSON, XML) rather than directly with the resources themselves.

Self-descriptive messages: Each message includes enough information to describe how to process it.

Hypermedia as the engine of application state (HATEOAS): Responses include links to related resources, allowing clients to dynamically navigate the API.

Layered System: The client doesn't need to know the internal implementation of the server. Intermediary servers can be used to improve scalability and security.

Code on Demand (Optional): Servers can temporarily extend or customize the functionality of a client by transferring executable code (e.g., JavaScript).

3. Designing RESTful APIs:

Resource Naming: Use nouns to represent resources (e.g., `/users`, `/products`) and keep URIs clear and concise.

HTTP Methods:

`GET`: Retrieve a resource or a collection of resources.

`POST`: Create a new resource.

`PUT`: Update an existing resource.

`DELETE`: Delete a resource.

Status Codes: Use appropriate HTTP status codes to indicate the outcome of requests (e.g., `200 OK`, `201 Created`, `404 Not Found`, `500 Internal Server Error`).

Data Formats: Use common data formats like JSON (JavaScript Object Notation) for exchanging data between the client and server.

4. Benefits of RESTful APIs:

Scalability: RESTful APIs are stateless, making them easier to scale to handle a large number of requests.

Flexibility: Clients and servers can be developed and modified independently.

Interoperability: RESTful APIs use standard HTTP methods and data formats, making them compatible with a wide range of clients and programming languages.

6.2 Creating API Endpoints with Go

This section provides a hands-on guide to building RESTful API endpoints using Go and the `net/http` package.

1. Defining Routes:

`http.HandleFunc()`: Use the `http.HandleFunc()` function to map HTTP requests to specific handler functions based on the URL path and HTTP method.

Example:

Go

```
http.HandleFunc("/users",        getUsersHandler)
// GET /users
```

```
http.HandleFunc("/users",
createUserHandler).Methods("POST") // POST /users

http.HandleFunc("/users/{id}",
getUserHandler).Methods("GET")            //       GET
/users/{id}
```

2. Handling Requests:

Handler Functions: Write handler functions that take an `http.ResponseWriter` and an `http.Request` as arguments. These functions will process the incoming requests and generate the API responses.

Example:

Go

```go
func   getUsersHandler(w   http.ResponseWriter,   r
*http.Request) {

    // ... retrieve users from the database ...

            w.Header().Set("Content-Type",
"application/json")

    json.NewEncoder(w).Encode(users)

}
```

3. Processing Request Data:

`r.Body`: Access the request body using `r.Body` for POST or PUT requests.

Decoding JSON: Use the `json.NewDecoder(r.Body).Decode(&data)` to decode JSON data from the request body into a Go struct.

Example:

Go

```go
func createUserHandler(w http.ResponseWriter, r *http.Request) {

    var user User

    err := json.NewDecoder(r.Body).Decode(&user)

    if err != nil {

        http.Error(w, "Invalid request data", http.StatusBadRequest)

        return

    }

    // ... store the user in the database ...

    w.WriteHeader(http.StatusCreated)

}
```

4. Generating Responses:

`w.Header().Set()`: Set response headers (e.g., `Content-Type`).

`w.WriteHeader()`: Set the HTTP status code (e.g., `http.StatusOK`, `http.StatusCreated`).

`json.NewEncoder(w).Encode()`: Encode data as JSON and send it in the response body.

Example:

Go

```go
func getUserHandler(w http.ResponseWriter, r *http.Request) {

    // ... retrieve user from the database ...

    if user == nil {

            http.Error(w, "User not found", http.StatusNotFound)

        return

    }

            w.Header().Set("Content-Type", "application/json")

    json.NewEncoder(w).Encode(user)

}
```

5. Error Handling:

`http.Error()`: Use `http.Error()` to send error responses with appropriate status codes and messages.

Custom Error Responses: Create custom error structs to provide more detailed error information in the API response.

6. Routing Libraries:

Gorilla Mux: Introduce Gorilla Mux (`github.com/gorilla/mux`) as a popular routing library that provides more advanced features like parameterized routes, middleware, and subrouters.

Example with Gorilla Mux:

Go

```go
import (

    "github.com/gorilla/mux"

)



func main() {

    router := mux.NewRouter()

                router.HandleFunc("/users",
getUsersHandler).Methods("GET")

    // ... other routes ...

    http.ListenAndServe(":8080", router)

}
```

6.3 Handling JSON Data with Encoding/Decoding

This section focuses on working with JSON (JavaScript Object Notation), a common data format for APIs, and how to encode and decode JSON data in your Go web applications.

1. What is JSON?

Data Interchange Format: JSON is a lightweight, text-based data format that is easy for humans to read and write and easy for machines to parse and generate. It is widely used for data exchange on the web, especially in APIs.

Structure: JSON data is structured as key-value pairs, where keys are strings and values can be strings, numbers, booleans, arrays, or other JSON objects.

Example:

JSON

```json
{

  "name": "Alice",

  "email": "alice@example.com",

  "age": 30,

  "active": true,

  "address": {

    "street": "123 Main St",

    "city": "Anytown"

  }
```

```
}
```

2. Encoding JSON Data in Go:

`encoding/json` **Package:** Go's standard library provides the `encoding/json` package for encoding and decoding JSON data.

`json.Marshal()`: Use the `json.Marshal()` function to encode Go data structures (structs, maps, slices) into JSON data.

Example:

Go

```go
type User struct {

    Name  string `json:"name"`

    Email string `json:"email"`

    Age   int    `json:"age"`

}



func main() {

        user := User{Name: "Alice", Email: "alice@example.com", Age: 30}

    jsonData, err := json.Marshal(user)

    if err != nil {

        // Handle error
```

```go
    }

        fmt.Println(string(jsonData))  // Output:
{"name":"Alice","email":"alice@example.com","age"
:30}

}
```

3. Decoding JSON Data in Go:

`json.Unmarshal()`: Use the `json.Unmarshal()` function to decode JSON data into Go data structures.

Example:

Go

```go
func main() {

                                jsonData        :=
[]byte(`{"name":"Bob","email":"bob@example.com","
age":25}`)

    var user User

    err := json.Unmarshal(jsonData, &user)

    if err != nil {

        // Handle error

    }

    fmt.Println(user.Name) // Output: Bob

}
```

4. Working with APIs:

Sending JSON in Requests: When sending data to an API in a `POST` or `PUT` request, set the `Content-Type` header to `application/json` and encode the data as JSON using `json.Marshal()`.

Receiving JSON in Responses: When receiving JSON data from an API, decode the response body using `json.Unmarshal()`.

5. Customizing JSON Encoding/Decoding:

JSON Tags: Use JSON tags in your Go structs to control how the fields are encoded and decoded (e.g., change field names, omit empty fields).

Custom Marshalers/Unmarshalers: Implement the `json.Marshaler` and `json.Unmarshaler` interfaces for more complex encoding/decoding logic.

6. Best Practices:

Error Handling: Always handle potential errors during encoding and decoding.

Data Validation: Validate JSON data after decoding to ensure it meets your application's requirements.

By mastering JSON encoding and decoding in Go, your readers will be able to effectively work with APIs and handle JSON data in their web applications.

Chapter 7

Authentication and Authorization

7.1 Implementing User Login and Registration

1. User Registration:

Registration Form: Create an HTML form that collects the necessary user information (e.g., username, email, password).

Handling Form Submission: In your Go handler function:

Retrieve the form data using `r.FormValue()`.

Hash the Password: Never store passwords in plain text. Use a strong hashing algorithm like bcrypt to hash the password before storing it in the database.

Create User Record: Store the user information (including the hashed password) in your database.

Generate Confirmation Email (Optional): Send a confirmation email to the user's email address to verify their account.

Example (Registration Handler):

Go

```go
func registerHandler(w http.ResponseWriter, r *http.Request) {

    if r.Method == http.MethodPost {

        // ... retrieve form data ...
```

```go
                    hashedPassword,    err    :=
bcrypt.GenerateFromPassword([]byte(password),
bcrypt.DefaultCost)

        if err != nil {

            // Handle error

        }

        // ... create user record in the database
with hashedPassword ...

    } else {

        // ... display the registration form ...

    }

}
```

2. User Login:

Login Form: Create an HTML form for users to enter their username/email and password.

Handling Login: In your Go handler function:

Retrieve the entered username/email and password.

Retrieve User Record: Query the database for a user with the given username/email.

Compare Passwords: Use `bcrypt.CompareHashAndPassword()` to compare the entered password with the stored hashed password.

Generate Session: If the passwords match, generate a session for the user (more on this in the next section).

Redirect: Redirect the user to the appropriate page (e.g., their profile page, the home page).

Example (Login Handler):

Go

```go
func    loginHandler(w    http.ResponseWriter,    r
*http.Request) {

    if r.Method == http.MethodPost {

        // ... retrieve username/email and
password ...

        // ... retrieve user record from the
database ...

                                    err    :=
bcrypt.CompareHashAndPassword(hashedPassword,
[]byte(password))

        if err != nil {

        // Invalid password

        }

        // ... generate session ...

                    http.Redirect(w,    r,    "/",
http.StatusSeeOther)

    } else {

        // ... display the login form ...
```

}

}

3. Security Considerations:

Password Hashing: Emphasize the importance of hashing passwords using strong algorithms like bcrypt.

Input Validation: Validate all user input to prevent injection attacks and other vulnerabilities.

HTTPS: Always use HTTPS to protect user credentials during transmission.

Rate Limiting: Implement rate limiting to prevent brute-force attacks.

Password Complexity: Enforce password complexity rules (minimum length, required characters).

4. Third-Party Authentication:

OAuth: Briefly mention OAuth and OpenID Connect as options for allowing users to log in with their existing accounts from providers like Google, Facebook, or GitHub.

7.2 Session Management and Cookies

This section explains how to manage user sessions and utilize cookies to maintain user authentication across multiple requests in your Go web applications.

1. What are Sessions?

Concept: A session is a way to store user-specific data on the server-side, allowing you to track and maintain the user's state across multiple requests. This is crucial for features like user login, shopping carts, and personalized content.

Session ID: Each session is associated with a unique identifier (session ID), which is typically sent to the client (browser) and stored in a cookie.

Server-Side Storage: The actual session data (e.g., user ID, login status, shopping cart items) is stored on the server, often in a database or in memory.

2. Cookies in Go:

`net/http` **Package:** The `net/http` package provides functions for working with cookies:

`http.SetCookie(w, &http.Cookie)`: Sets a cookie in the HTTP response.

`r.Cookie("cookieName")`: Retrieves a cookie from the HTTP request.

- **Cookie Attributes:**

Name: The name of the cookie.

Value: The value of the cookie.

Expires: The expiration date of the cookie.

Path: The URL path where the cookie is valid.

Domain: The domain where the cookie is valid.

Secure: Specifies whether the cookie should only be transmitted over HTTPS.

HttpOnly: Prevents client-side JavaScript from accessing the cookie, enhancing security.

3. Session Management in Go:

Libraries: Several libraries simplify session management in Go, such as:

1 Gorilla Sessions: (`github.com/gorilla/sessions`) Provides various session stores (in-memory, file system, database).

2 scs: (`github.com/alexedwards/scs`) A lightweight and secure session management library.

Steps:

1 Generate Session ID: Generate a unique session ID when the user logs in.

2 Store Session Data: Store the session data (e.g., user ID) on the server, associated with the session ID.

3 Set Cookie: Set a cookie in the HTTP response containing the session ID.

4 Retrieve Session: On subsequent requests, retrieve the session ID from the cookie and use it to load the session data from the server.

4. Example (Gorilla Sessions):

Go

```go
import (

    "github.com/gorilla/sessions"

)
```

```go
var                    store                    =
sessions.NewCookieStore([]byte("your-secret-key")
)


func    loginHandler(w    http.ResponseWriter,    r
*http.Request) {

    // ... authenticate user ...

    session, _ := store.Get(r, "my-session")

    session.Values["user_id"] = user.ID

    session.Save(r, w)

}


func    profileHandler(w    http.ResponseWriter,    r
*http.Request) {

    session, _ := store.Get(r, "my-session")

    userID := session.Values["user_id"]

    // ... retrieve user data based on userID ...

}
```

5. Security Considerations:

Secure Cookies: Always set the `Secure` flag for cookies in production environments to ensure they are only transmitted over HTTPS.

HttpOnly Cookies: Set the `HttpOnly` flag to prevent client-side JavaScript from accessing sensitive cookies.

Session Fixation: Implement measures to prevent session fixation attacks, where an attacker tricks a user into using a known session ID.

Session Expiration: Set appropriate session expiration times to limit the duration of user sessions.

7.3 Securing Your Go Web Applications

1. Secure Coding Practices:

Input Validation: Always validate and sanitize all user input to prevent injection attacks (SQL injection, Cross-Site Scripting) and other vulnerabilities.

Output Encoding: Encode data dynamically displayed on web pages to prevent Cross-Site Scripting (XSS) attacks.

Error Handling: Handle errors gracefully and avoid revealing sensitive information in error messages.

Third-Party Libraries: Use well-maintained and secure third-party libraries. Keep them updated to patch known vulnerabilities.

Code Reviews: Conduct regular code reviews to identify potential security issues.

2. Authentication and Authorization:

Strong Passwords: Enforce strong password policies (minimum length, complexity requirements).

Hashing: Always hash passwords using strong, one-way hashing algorithms like bcrypt. Never store passwords in plain text.

Multi-Factor Authentication (MFA): Consider implementing MFA to add an extra layer of security.

Authorization: Implement proper authorization mechanisms to control access to resources based on user roles and permissions.

3. Session Management:

Secure Cookies: Use HTTPS to protect cookies during transmission. Set the `Secure` and `HttpOnly` flags for cookies.

Session Expiration: Set appropriate session expiration times to limit the duration of user sessions.

Session Fixation: Prevent session fixation attacks by regenerating session IDs after login.

4. Cross-Site Request Forgery (CSRF) Protection:

CSRF Tokens: Use CSRF tokens to prevent CSRF attacks. Include a unique, unpredictable token in each form submission and validate it on the server-side.

Double Submit Cookies: Another technique for CSRF protection involves setting a cookie with a random value and including the same value as a hidden field in the form.

5. API Security:

Authentication: Secure APIs using appropriate authentication methods (e.g., API keys, OAuth 2.0).

Rate Limiting: Implement rate limiting to prevent abuse and denial-of-service attacks.

Input Validation: Validate all API requests to ensure they meet the expected format and data types.

6. Deployment Security:

HTTPS: Always use HTTPS in production to encrypt communication between the client and server.

Web Application Firewall (WAF): Consider using a WAF to protect your application from common web attacks.

Secure Headers: Use security headers like `Content-Security-Policy`, `Strict-Transport-Security`, and `X-Frame-Options` to enhance browser security.

7. Security Tools and Resources:

Go Vulnerability Database: Use the Go Vulnerability Database to check for known vulnerabilities in your Go packages.

Static Analysis Tools: Use static analysis tools like `gosec` to identify potential security issues in your code.

OWASP: Refer to the Open Web Application Security Project (OWASP) for security guidelines and best practices.

Chapter 8

Go Web Frameworks

8.1 Introduction to Popular Go Web Frameworks (Gin, Echo, Fiber)

1. Why Use a Web Framework?

Efficiency: Frameworks provide pre-built components and utilities for common web development tasks (routing, middleware, templating), saving you time and effort.

Structure: Frameworks encourage a more organized and structured approach to building web applications.

Features: Frameworks often offer additional features like data validation, error handling, and security enhancements.

2. Gin:

Lightweight and Fast: Gin is known for its minimalist design and high performance. It's a good choice for building APIs and microservices.

Features:

Martini-like API: Gin's API is inspired by the Martini framework, making it easy to learn and use.

Middleware Support: Easily add middleware for logging, authentication, authorization, etc.

Built-in Rendering: Supports various template engines.

JSON Validation: Provides convenient functions for validating JSON data.

Example:

Go

```go
import "github.com/gin-gonic/gin"

func main() {

    router := gin.Default()

    router.GET("/ping", func(c *gin.Context) {

        c.JSON(200, gin.H{

            "message": "pong",

        })

    })

        router.Run() // listen and serve on
0.0.0.0:8080

}
```

3. Echo:

High Performance: Echo boasts a fast and efficient HTTP router.

Features:

Extensible: Highly modular and customizable.

Middleware: Supports middleware for various functionalities.

Data Binding: Binds request data to Go structs.

Template Rendering: Supports different template engines.

Example:

Go

```go
import (

    "net/http"


    "github.com/labstack/echo/v4"

)



func main() {

    e := echo.New()

    e.GET("/", func(c echo.Context) error {

        return c.String(http.StatusOK, "Hello,
World!")

    })

    e.Logger.Fatal(e.Start(":1323"))

}
```

4. Fiber:

Express.js Inspired: Fiber's API is heavily inspired by Express.js, a popular Node.js framework.

Features:

Fast: Claims to be one of the fastest Go web frameworks.

Lightweight: Minimalistic design with a small memory footprint.

Easy to Use: Simple and intuitive API.

Middleware Support: Supports middleware for various functionalities.

Example:

Go

```go
import "github.com/gofiber/fiber/v2"


func main() {

    app := fiber.New()


    app.Get("/", func(c *fiber.Ctx) error {

        return c.SendString("Hello, World!")

    })


    app.Listen(":3000")

}
```

5. Choosing a Framework:

Project Needs: Consider the specific needs of your project (performance, scalability, features).

Learning Curve: Evaluate the learning curve and ease of use of each framework.

Community Support: Choose a framework with active community support and good documentation.

8.2 Building a Web App with a Framework (Choosing One, Project Setup)

This section guides your readers through the process of choosing a Go web framework and setting up a new web application project.

1. Choosing a Framework:

Recap: Briefly recap the popular Go web frameworks introduced in the previous section (Gin, Echo, Fiber) and their key features.

Decision Factors: Guide readers in choosing a framework based on their project's needs and preferences:

Project Type: Is it an API, a web application with server-side rendering, or a single-page application?

Performance: How important is raw performance and low latency?

Features: Does the framework provide the necessary features (routing, middleware, templating, data validation)?

Learning Curve: How easy is it to learn and use the framework?

Community Support: Is there an active community and good documentation?

Recommendation: For this example, let's choose **Gin** due to its popularity, performance, and ease of use.

2. Project Setup:

Create Project Directory: Guide readers in creating a new directory for their project (e.g., `my-web-app`).

Initialize Go Modules: Use `go mod init` `github.com/your-username/my-web-app` (replace with your actual module path) to initialize a new Go module.

Install Gin: Use `go get github.com/gin-gonic/gin` to install the Gin framework.

Create `main.go`: Create a `main.go` file in the project directory.

Basic Gin Setup: Show the basic setup for a Gin application:

Go

```go
package main


import (

    "github.com/gin-gonic/gin"

)


func main() {

    router := gin.Default()

    router.GET("/", func(c *gin.Context) {
```

```
        c.String(200, "Hello, World!")

    })

    router.Run(":8080")

}
```

3. Directory Structure:

Organize Code: Suggest a basic directory structure for organizing the application code:

```
my-web-app/

├── controllers/    // Handlers for different routes

├── models/         // Data structures and database interactions

├── views/              // Templates (if using server-side rendering)

├── main.go         // Main application file

└── go.mod          // Go module file
```

4. Running the Application:

go run main.go: Show how to run the application using go run main.go.

Test in Browser: Access the application in a web browser at `http://localhost:8080`.

5. Next Steps:

Building Features: Guide readers on how to build specific features of their web application (e.g., user authentication, data storage, API endpoints) using the chosen framework.

8.3 Framework-Specific Features and Benefits

This section dives deeper into the specific features and benefits that each of the introduced Go web frameworks (Gin, Echo, and Fiber) offers.

1. Gin

Middleware: Gin excels in middleware support, allowing you to easily incorporate functions that execute before or after your route handlers. This is useful for:

Authentication: Verify user identity before granting access to protected routes.

Authorization: Control access to resources based on user roles and permissions.

Logging: Log requests and responses for debugging and monitoring.

Error Handling: Handle errors gracefully and provide consistent error responses.

Grouping and Routing: Gin allows you to group routes and apply middleware to entire groups, improving code organization and reducing redundancy.

Customizable Engine: Gin provides a highly customizable engine, allowing you to configure various aspects of the framework to suit your needs.

JSON Validation: Gin has built-in helpers for validating JSON request data, simplifying input validation.

2. Echo

HTTP/2 Support: Echo has excellent support for HTTP/2, the latest version of the HTTP protocol, which offers performance improvements and new features.

Data Binding: Echo simplifies data binding by automatically mapping request data (from forms, JSON, or query parameters) to Go structs.

Extensibility: Echo is highly extensible, allowing you to customize its behavior with middleware, renderers, and other components.

Centralized HTTP Error Handling: Echo provides a centralized mechanism for handling HTTP errors, making it easy to provide consistent error responses.

3. Fiber

Built-in Template Engine: Fiber includes a built-in template engine, making it easy to render dynamic HTML pages.

WebSocket Support: Fiber has built-in support for WebSockets, enabling real-time communication between your server and clients.

Static File Serving: Fiber simplifies serving static files (HTML, CSS, JavaScript, images) with its built-in static file server.

Fast and Efficient: Fiber is designed for speed and efficiency, making it a good choice for high-performance web applications.

Comparing Features:

Feature	Gin	Echo	Fiber
Performance	Excellent	Excellent	Excellent
Middleware	Excellent	Very good	Very good
Routing	Very good	Very good	Good
Data Binding	Good	Excellent	Good
Templating	Supports various engines	Supports various engines	Built-in engine
HTTP/2	Supported	Excellent support	Supported
WebSockets	Requires extension	Requires extension	Built-in support
Static File Serving	Easy	Easy	Built-in

Choosing the Right Framework:

Reiterate: Reiterate that the best framework depends on the specific needs and priorities of the project.

Trade-offs: Highlight that each framework has its own strengths and weaknesses, and choosing one often involves trade-offs.

By understanding the specific features and benefits of each framework, your readers can make informed decisions about which one to use for their Go web development projects.

Chapter 9

Testing and Debugging Go Web Apps

9.1 Writing Unit Tests for Go Web Code

1. Why Unit Testing?

Early Bug Detection: Unit tests help identify bugs early in the development process, making them easier and cheaper to fix.

Improved Code Quality: Writing testable code often leads to better design and more modular code.

Confidence in Changes: Unit tests provide a safety net when refactoring or adding new features, ensuring that existing functionality is not broken.

Documentation: Well-written tests serve as documentation, demonstrating how the code is intended to be used.

2. Go's `testing` Package:

Built-in Support: Go has built-in support for unit testing through the `testing` package.

Test Files: Test files are named with the `_test.go` suffix (e.g., `my_handler_test.go`).

Test Functions: Test functions start with the `Test` prefix and take a `*testing.T` argument (e.g., `func TestMyHandler(t *testing.T)`).

3. Testing Web Handlers:

`httptest` **Package:** The `net/http/httptest` package provides tools for testing HTTP handlers without running a full web server.

`httptest.NewRecorder()`: Creates a new `httptest.ResponseRecorder` to record the handler's response.

`httptest.NewRequest()`: Creates a new `httptest.Request` to simulate an HTTP request.

Example:

Go

```
package main

import (

    "net/http"

    "net/http/httptest"

    "testing"

)


func myHandler(w http.ResponseWriter, r *http.Request) {

    w.Write([]byte("Hello, World!"))

}
```

```go
func TestMyHandler(t *testing.T) {

    req := httptest.NewRequest("GET", "/", nil)

    w := httptest.NewRecorder()

    myHandler(w, req)


    if w.Code != http.StatusOK {

        t.Errorf("Expected status code %d, got %d", http.StatusOK, w.Code)

    }

    if w.Body.String() != "Hello, World!" {

        t.Errorf("Expected body %q, got %q", "Hello, World!", w.Body.String())

    }

}
```

4. Testing with Mock Objects:

Concept: Mock objects are simulated dependencies that mimic the behavior of real objects in a controlled way. This allows you to isolate the code under test and focus on its specific logic.

Example: If your handler interacts with a database, you can create a mock database object that returns predefined data for your tests.

5. Table-Driven Tests:

Concept: Table-driven tests allow you to test multiple scenarios with a single test function, improving code reuse and readability.

Example:

```Go
func TestMyHandler(t *testing.T) {

    tests := []struct {

        name        string

        method      string

        path        string

        wantCode    int

        wantBody    string

    }{

        {"GET /", "GET", "/", http.StatusOK,
"Hello, World!"},

        // ... more test cases ...

    }

    for _, tt := range tests {

        t.Run(tt.name, func(t *testing.T) {

            // ... create request and recorder
...

            myHandler(w, req)
```

```
                // ... assert response code and body
   ...


        })

     }

 }
```

6. Test Coverage:

`go test -cover`: Use the `-cover` flag with `go test` to generate a test coverage report. This shows how much of your code is covered by your tests.

9.2 Debugging Techniques and Tools

1. Basic Debugging Techniques:

Print Statements: The classic debugging technique involves adding `fmt.Println()` statements to your code to inspect variable values, program flow, and function outputs. This helps you understand what's happening at various points in your application.

Logging: Use a logging library (e.g., `log`, `logrus`) to record events, errors, and other relevant information. This provides a more structured and organized way to track down issues.

Code Comments: Temporarily comment out sections of code to isolate the source of a problem. This helps you narrow down the potential causes.

Read the Error Messages: Pay close attention to the error messages Go provides. They often contain valuable clues about the nature and location of the error.

2. Debugging Tools:

Delve: Delve is a powerful debugger for Go. It allows you to:

Set breakpoints: Pause execution at specific lines of code.

Step through code: Execute code line by line, observing variable values and program flow.

Inspect variables: Examine the values of variables at any point during execution.

Evaluate expressions: Evaluate Go expressions in the current context.

IDE Debuggers: Most IDEs (Integrated Development Environments) like VS Code and GoLand have built-in debuggers that provide similar functionalities to Delve.

Browser Developer Tools: Use your browser's developer tools (Network tab) to inspect HTTP requests and responses, analyze network activity, and identify frontend issues.

3. Debugging Tips:

Reproduce the Error: Before you start debugging, try to consistently reproduce the error. This helps you understand the conditions under which it occurs.

Isolate the Problem: Use techniques like print statements or commenting out code to isolate the specific part of your code that is causing the issue.

Test with Different Inputs: Try different input values to see if the error is related to specific data or conditions.

Simplify the Code: If possible, simplify the code around the error to make it easier to understand and debug.

Ask for Help: Don't hesitate to ask for help from other developers or online communities.

4. Debugging with Delve (Example):

Installation: `go get github.com/go-delve/delve/cmd/dlv`

Start Debugging: `dlv debug main.go`

Set Breakpoints: `break main.go:10` (sets a breakpoint at line 10 in `main.go`)

Continue Execution: `continue`

Step Over: `next`

Step Into: `step`

Print Variable: `print myVariable`

5. Using Browser Developer Tools:

Network Tab: Inspect HTTP requests and responses, view headers, response times, and data.

Console: View JavaScript errors and log messages.

Debugger: Debug JavaScript code running in the browser.

9.3 Performance Optimization and Profiling

This section focuses on techniques and tools to analyze and optimize the performance of your Go web applications.

1. Why Optimize Performance?

User Experience: Fast and responsive applications provide a better user experience, leading to increased user satisfaction and engagement.

Scalability: Optimized applications can handle more traffic and users with fewer resources.

Cost Efficiency: Reduced resource usage can translate to lower server costs and improved efficiency.

2. Profiling:

Concept: Profiling is the process of analyzing your application's performance to identify bottlenecks and areas for improvement. It helps you understand where your application spends its time and resources.

Types of Profiling:

CPU Profiling: Measures how much time is spent executing different parts of your code.

Memory Profiling: Tracks memory allocation and usage to identify memory leaks and inefficient memory management.

Blocking Profiling: Identifies areas where goroutines are blocked, waiting for resources (e.g., I/O operations, locks).

3. Go Profiling Tools:

`pprof`: Go's built-in profiling tool, `pprof`, provides detailed performance profiles that can be visualized and analyzed.

Enable Profiling: Import the `net/http/pprof` package and register its handlers in your application.

Access Profiles: Access profiles through a web interface (e.g., `http://localhost:8080/debug/pprof/`) or use the `go tool pprof` command-line tool.

Tracing: Go also provides tracing capabilities to analyze the execution of goroutines and identify performance issues related to concurrency.

4. Performance Optimization Techniques:

Efficient Data Structures and Algorithms: Choose appropriate data structures and algorithms for your tasks. Consider time and space complexity when making decisions.

Concurrency: Use Go's concurrency features (goroutines, channels) effectively to parallelize tasks and improve performance. Avoid race conditions and deadlocks.

Database Optimization: Optimize database queries, use indexes, and consider caching to reduce database load.

Caching: Implement caching mechanisms to store frequently accessed data in memory, reducing the need for repeated computations or database queries.

Asynchronous Operations: Use asynchronous operations for tasks that don't need to be performed synchronously, such as sending emails or processing background jobs.

Code Optimization: Review and optimize your code for efficiency. Avoid unnecessary computations, reduce function calls, and optimize loops.

HTTP/2: Use HTTP/2 to improve network performance with features like multiplexing and header compression.

Gzip Compression: Enable Gzip compression to reduce the size of HTTP responses, improving loading times.

5. Analyzing Profiles:

Visualizations: Use `pprof`'s visualization tools (e.g., `go tool pprof -http=:8081`) to analyze CPU and memory profiles.

Identify Bottlenecks: Look for functions or code sections that consume a significant amount of time or memory.

Focus on Hotspots: Prioritize optimizing the areas that have the biggest impact on performance.

6. Benchmarking:

`testing` **Package:** Use Go's `testing` package to write benchmarks that measure the performance of specific functions or code blocks.

Example:

Go

```go
func BenchmarkMyFunction(b *testing.B) {

    for i := 0; i < b.N; i++ {

        MyFunction()

    }

}
```

By incorporating these performance optimization techniques and profiling tools, your readers can ensure their Go web applications are fast, efficient, and scalable.

Chapter 10

Deployment and Scaling

10.1 Deploying Go Web Apps to Servers (Cloud Platforms, Docker)

1. Traditional Server Deployment:

Server Setup:

Choose a server provider (e.g., DigitalOcean, AWS, Google Cloud).

Select a server with appropriate resources (CPU, memory, storage) based on your application's needs.

Install Go on the server.

Set up necessary dependencies (e.g., database, web server).

Building the Application:

Use `go build` to compile your Go application into an executable binary.

Transfer the binary to the server.

Running the Application:

Use a process manager (e.g., systemd, supervisor) to run the application as a background process.

Configure a web server (e.g., Nginx, Apache) to act as a reverse proxy, forwarding requests to your Go application.

Example (systemd):

```
[Unit]
```

```
Description=My Go Web App

After=network.target


[Service]

User=myuser

WorkingDirectory=/home/myuser/my-web-app

ExecStart=/home/myuser/my-web-app/my-app

Restart=always


[Install]

WantedBy=multi-user.target
```

2. Docker Deployment:

Docker Basics:

Briefly introduce Docker and its benefits (portability, consistency, isolation).

Explain the concepts of Docker images and containers.

Creating a Dockerfile:

Guide readers in creating a `Dockerfile` to define the environment and build their Go application within a Docker image.

Example `Dockerfile`:

Dockerfile

```
FROM golang:latest

WORKDIR /app

COPY go.mod ./
COPY go.sum ./
RUN go mod download

COPY . .
RUN go build -o my-app

EXPOSE 8080

CMD ["./my-app"]
```

Building the Docker Image:

Use `docker build -t my-web-app .` to build the Docker image.

Running the Docker Container:

Use `docker run -p 8080:8080 my-web-app` to run the application in a Docker container.

Docker Compose:

Introduce Docker Compose for managing multi-container applications.

Example `docker-compose.yml`:

YAML

```yaml
version: "3.9"

services:

  web:

    build: .

    ports:

      - "8080:8080"

  db:

    image: postgres:latest

    environment:

      POSTGRES_PASSWORD: mysecretpassword
```

3. Cloud Platform Deployment:

Cloud Providers:

Discuss popular cloud platforms like AWS (Elastic Beanstalk, ECS), Google Cloud (App Engine, Cloud Run), and Azure (App Service).

Highlight the benefits of using cloud platforms (scalability, reliability, managed services).

Deployment Methods:

Explain different deployment methods:

Deploying Docker containers: Most cloud platforms support deploying Dockerized applications.

Platform-specific tools: Cloud providers offer tools and services to simplify deployments.

Example (Deploying to Google Cloud Run with Docker):

Build the Docker image.

Push the image to Google Container Registry (GCR).

Deploy the image to Cloud Run using the `gcloud` command-line tool.

4. Deployment Best Practices:

Continuous Integration/Continuous Deployment (CI/CD): Use CI/CD pipelines to automate the build, test, and deployment process.

Environment Variables: Use environment variables to store sensitive information and configure your application for different environments.

Monitoring and Logging: Set up monitoring and logging to track application performance and identify potential issues.

10.2 Scaling for High Traffic and Performance

This section delves into strategies and techniques for scaling your Go web applications to handle high traffic loads and maintain optimal performance.

1. Understanding Scalability

Definition: Scalability refers to an application's ability to handle increasing amounts of traffic and data without sacrificing performance.

Why it Matters: As your user base grows, your application needs to handle more requests, data, and complexity. Scalability ensures your application remains responsive and reliable even under heavy load.

2. Vertical Scaling (Scaling Up)

Concept: Vertical scaling involves increasing the resources of a single server (e.g., more CPU, memory, storage).

Limitations: Vertical scaling has limits as server resources are finite. It can also lead to a single point of failure.

3. Horizontal Scaling (Scaling Out)

Concept: Horizontal scaling involves adding more servers to distribute the load. This is generally more scalable and fault-tolerant.

Load Balancing: Load balancers distribute incoming traffic across multiple servers, preventing any single server from becoming overwhelmed.

Types of Load Balancers:

Hardware Load Balancers: Physical devices that distribute traffic.

Software Load Balancers: Software applications that run on servers (e.g., Nginx, HAProxy).

Cloud Load Balancers: Services provided by cloud providers (e.g., AWS Elastic Load Balancing, Google Cloud Load Balancing).

4. Database Scaling

Scaling Databases: Databases can become bottlenecks as data grows and queries increase.

Techniques:

Read Replicas: Use read replicas to handle read-heavy workloads.

Sharding: Divide your database into smaller, more manageable chunks (shards) distributed across multiple servers.

Caching: Cache frequently accessed data to reduce database load.

5. Caching

Concept: Caching involves storing frequently accessed data in a fast, easily accessible location (e.g., in-memory, Redis).

Benefits: Reduced database load, faster response times, improved performance.

Types of Caching:

Server-Side Caching: Cache data on the server-side (e.g., in memory, Redis, Memcached).

Client-Side Caching: Cache data on the client-side (e.g., browser cache).

Content Delivery Network (CDN): Distribute static content (images, CSS, JavaScript) globally to reduce latency.

6. Asynchronous Processing

Concept: Offload time-consuming tasks (e.g., sending emails, processing images) to background workers or queues.

Benefits: Improved responsiveness, reduced request processing time, better user experience.

Tools: Use message queues (e.g., RabbitMQ, Kafka) or task queues (e.g., Celery) for asynchronous processing.

7. Microservices

Concept: Break down your application into smaller, independent services that communicate with each other.

Benefits: Improved scalability, maintainability, and fault isolation.

Challenges: Increased complexity in managing and coordinating multiple services.

8. Go-Specific Considerations

Concurrency: Leverage Go's concurrency features (goroutines, channels) to handle concurrent requests efficiently.

Efficient Code: Write optimized and efficient code to minimize resource usage.

9. Monitoring and Performance Testing

Monitoring: Use monitoring tools (e.g., Prometheus, Grafana) to track key metrics (e.g., request latency, error rates, resource usage).

Performance Testing: Conduct performance tests (e.g., load testing, stress testing) to identify bottlenecks and ensure your application can handle expected traffic.

10.3 Scaling for High Traffic and Performance

This section delves into strategies and techniques for scaling your Go web applications to handle high traffic loads and maintain optimal performance.

1. Understanding Scalability

Definition: Scalability refers to an application's ability to handle increasing amounts of traffic and data without sacrificing performance.

Why it Matters: As your user base grows, your application needs to handle more requests, data, and complexity. Scalability ensures your application remains responsive and reliable even under heavy load.

2. Vertical Scaling (Scaling Up)

Concept: Vertical scaling involves increasing the resources of a single server (e.g., more CPU, memory, storage).

Limitations: Vertical scaling has limits as server resources are finite. It can also lead to a single point of failure.

3. Horizontal Scaling (Scaling Out)

Concept: Horizontal scaling involves adding more servers to distribute the load. This is generally more scalable and fault-tolerant.

Load Balancing: Load balancers distribute incoming traffic across multiple servers, preventing any single server from becoming overwhelmed.

Types of Load Balancers:

Hardware Load Balancers: Physical devices that distribute traffic.

Software Load Balancers: Software applications that run on servers (e.g., Nginx, HAProxy).

Cloud Load Balancers: Services provided by cloud providers (e.g., AWS Elastic Load Balancing, Google Cloud Load Balancing).

4. Database Scaling

Scaling Databases: Databases can become bottlenecks as data grows and queries increase.

Techniques:

Read Replicas: Use read replicas to handle read-heavy workloads.

Sharding: Divide your database into smaller, more manageable chunks (shards) distributed across multiple servers.

Caching: Cache frequently accessed data to reduce database load.

5. Caching

Concept: Caching involves storing frequently accessed data in a fast, easily accessible location (e.g., in-memory, Redis).

Benefits: Reduced database load, faster response times, improved performance.

Types of Caching:

Server-Side Caching: Cache data on the server-side (e.g., in memory, Redis, Memcached).

Client-Side Caching: Cache data on the client-side (e.g., browser cache).

Content Delivery Network (CDN): Distribute static content (images, CSS, JavaScript) globally to reduce latency.

6. Asynchronous Processing

Concept: Offload time-consuming tasks (e.g., sending emails, processing images) to background workers or queues.

Benefits: Improved responsiveness, reduced request processing time, better user experience.

Tools: Use message queues (e.g., RabbitMQ, Kafka) or task queues (e.g., Celery) for asynchronous processing.

7. Microservices

Concept: Break down your application into smaller, independent services that communicate with each other.

Benefits: Improved scalability, maintainability, and fault isolation.

Challenges: Increased complexity in managing and coordinating multiple services.

8. Go-Specific Considerations

Concurrency: Leverage Go's concurrency features (goroutines, channels) to handle concurrent requests efficiently.

Efficient Code: Write optimized and efficient code to minimize resource usage.

9. Monitoring and Performance Testing

Monitoring: Use monitoring tools (e.g., Prometheus, Grafana) to track key metrics (e.g., request latency, error rates, resource usage).

Performance Testing: Conduct performance tests (e.g., load testing, stress testing) to identify bottlenecks and ensure your application can handle expected traffic.

www.ingramcontent.com/pod-product-compliance
Lightning Source LLC
LaVergne TN
LVHW051738050326
832903LV00023B/996